D0794587

DOG OBEDIENCE

Getting Your Pooch Off the Couch and Other Dog Training Tips

By Liz Palika

CAPSTONE PRESS
a capstone imprint

Edge Books are published by Capstone Press,
151 Good Counsel Drive, P.O. Box 669, Mankato, Minnesota 56002.
www.capstonepub.com

 Books published by Capstone Press are manufactured with paper
containing at least 10 percent post-consumer waste.

Library of Congress Cataloging-in-Publication Data
Palika, Liz, 1954–
    Dog obedience : getting your pooch off the couch and other dog training tips /
        by Liz Palika.
        p. cm. — (Edge books. Dog ownership)
    Includes bibliographical references and index.
    Summary: "Describes tips and information on teaching obedience to dogs"—
        Provided by publisher.
    ISBN 978-1-4296-6525-4 (library binding)
    1. Dogs—Training—Juvenile literature. I. Title.
    SF431.P336 2012
    636.7'0887—dc22   2011003795

Editorial Credits

Angie Kaelberer, editor; Bobbie Nuytten and Ashlee Suker, designers;
    Marcie Spence, media researcher; Eric Manske, production specialist

Photo Credits

Alamy Images: People, 11, Capstone Studio: Karon Dubke, 5, 6, 7, 8, 9, 10,
12, 13, 14, 16, 18, 20, 21, 22, 23, 24, 25, 26, 27, 29, Shutterstock: AnetaPics, 1,
hd connelly, design element, Lisa Fischer, design element, Mike Flippo, cover,
Photosani, 17; stocksock, design element

Printed in the United States of America in Stevens Point, Wisconsin.
032011   006111WZF11

Table of Contents

COMMANDS

Before You Begin

Dogs have been our companions for thousands of years. They rush to greet us when we get home. They listen when we talk and snuggle when we need a hug.

But sometimes dogs' enthusiasm can also get them into trouble. A dog that jumps on people can hurt them. A dog that dashes out the door could get lost or be hit by a car.

By training your dog, you can teach him to be an even better friend and companion. Luckily, **obedience** training isn't difficult and can be a fun way for you and your dog to spend time together.

You may have already noticed that your dog recognizes some words. He may know that "ball" refers to his favorite toy and "outside" means to go into the backyard.

As you train your dog, he will learn more words. When you teach him to sit, he'll learn that "sit" means to put his rear on the ground. It's important to be consistent with your **commands**. If you change words, your dog will get confused.

obedience—following rules and commands
command—a word or phrase that tells a dog to do something

You will also need some things to help train your dog. Make sure your dog is wearing a collar. Before starting to teach your dog each day, hook up a leash to his collar. The leash will keep him close to you.

Some tasty treats will make training easier. Pieces of cheese or hot dogs are great training treats. When your dog learns the command well, you can stop using treats. But don't be in a hurry to stop using them. Just be careful that you aren't giving your dog so many treats that he becomes overweight.

A collar and leash are good dog training tools.

Try to practice training with your dog every day. Twice a day is even better. Most important, never yell at your dog, get angry with him, or hit him. Instead, keep the training fun so your dog wants to do what you ask.

Easy

Your dog's first lesson is to take things gently from your hand. A quick or rough grab could hurt you.

Step 1: Hold the leash in one hand. Have a treat in the other hand. Close your fingers around the treat so your hand forms a fist with your fingers facing up.

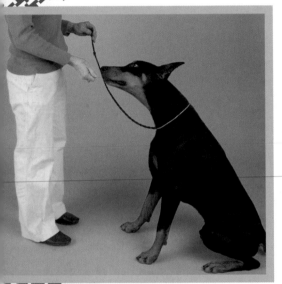

Step 2: Let your dog sniff your hand. He'll be able to smell the treat.

Step 3: In this book, we will use the example name of Buddy. As he's sniffing your hand, uncurl your fingers slowly, say his name, and then say, "Easy." Then let him lick the treat out of your hand. As he licks it out gently, **praise** him, "Good boy, Buddy!"

If your dog grabs for the treat, close your fingers and put your hand behind your back. When he's calm, start over with steps 1 through 3.

TRAINING TIP

If your dog ever growls at you or bites you, stop training right away and ask an adult for help.

praise—to say words of approval

Give

Does your dog like to play tug of war when he has something in his mouth—especially if it's something he shouldn't have? This command teaches him to give up something. You'll ask him to trade a toy for a treat.

Step 1: Let your dog drag his leash. Have one of your dog's favorite toys in one hand and a treat in the other hand.

Step 2: Play with your dog and his toy for a moment, and then show him the treat. If he drops the toy and reaches for the treat, tell him, "Buddy, give! Good boy!" Let him lick the treat out of your hand.

If your dog tries to run away with his toy, step on the leash to stop him. Then show him the treat again. Try putting the treat close to his nose so he smells it. Repeat the "give" command. Praise him when he drops the toy and takes the treat. When your dog learns this command well, you can stop using treats, but always praise him.

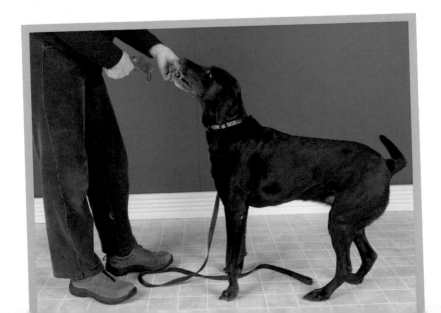

Sit

Some dogs just can't seem to hold still. It's hard to train a dog that is always wriggling. When your dog learns the "sit" command, he also learns to hold still.

Step 1: Face your dog. Take hold of the leash close to his collar. Have a treat in your other hand.

Step 2: Let your dog sniff the treat in your hand. As you say, "Buddy, sit," move the treat up over his head and then back toward his shoulders. He will lift his nose in the air to see where you're moving the treat.

Step 3: As his head comes up, his rear will move to the ground. Tell him, "Good boy, Buddy!" Let him lick the treat out of your hand.

TRAINING TIP

If your dog is confused, repeat all the steps. Make sure to move your hand with the treat very slowly so his nose can follow your hand.

All Done

The "sit" command teaches your dog how to be still. But your dog can't sit all the time. The "all done" command lets him know when he can move.

Step 1: Practice the "sit" command as shown on page 8, steps 1 through 3.

Step 2: After your dog licks the treat out of your hand, tell him, "Buddy, all done."

Step 3: Using the leash, walk him forward a couple of steps. Tell him, "Good boy, Buddy!"

By walking him forward, you're showing him that he's finished sitting for the moment. When you tell him "Good boy," you are letting him know it's OK to get up when you say "All done." Pet, praise, and play with your dog.

"Sit" and "all done" both teach good behavior to your dog. Ask your dog to sit any time you want to give him something good, like a treat or a toy. Tell him "all done" when he can move.

Ask your dog to sit before you feed him. When he's sitting nicely, he won't be able to knock the food bowl out of your hands. Tell him "all done" after you set the bowl on the floor.

TRAINING TIP

Some dogs are so excited to see people that they jump up on them. They don't know they can scratch people with their claws or knock them down. When your dog jumps up, turn your back on him. He wants your attention, so he will likely stop jumping.

Down

"Down" is a good command to use when you want your dog to settle down quietly.

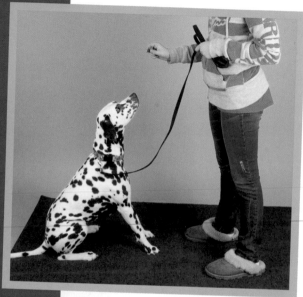

Step 1: Hold the leash in one hand. Have two treats in the other hand.

Step 2: Ask your dog to sit. Praise him for sitting and give him one treat.

Step 3: Let your dog sniff your hand holding the second treat.

Step 4: Move the hand with the treat slowly toward the ground. Your dog's nose should follow your hand. As he starts to lie down, tell him, "Buddy, down! Good!" If your dog isn't following, put the hand holding the leash on your dog's shoulder.

TRAINING TIP

If your dog is having trouble learning a command, try a different treat.

Step 5: When your dog is on the ground, let him lick the treat out of your hand. If he tries to get up, keep his leash close to the ground so he can't.

Step 6: After a few seconds, tell him, "Buddy, all done!" and encourage him to get up.

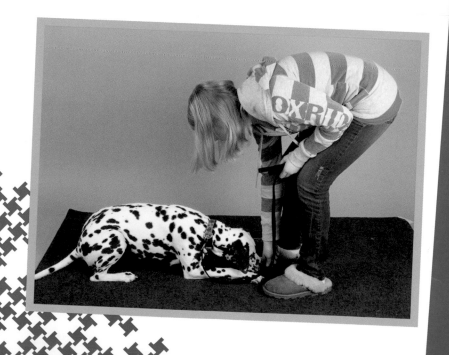

Stay

The "stay" command teaches your dog to remain in place when you walk away from him.

Step 1: Hold the leash with one hand. Have a treat in the other hand.

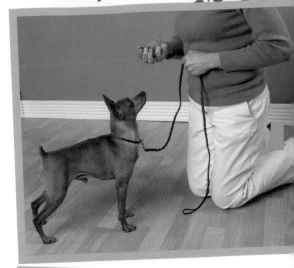

Step 2: Ask your dog to sit. When he does, praise him and give him the treat. Do not tell him, "All done."

Step 3: Extend your arm firmly, palm toward your dog's nose, as you tell him, "Buddy, stay."

Step 4: Take one step away from your dog. If he stays, give him the treat. If he gets up from the sit, say, "No." Tell him to sit and stay again.

Step 5: After he sits still for five seconds, step back to him. Praise him and tell him he can move by saying, "Buddy, all done!"

When your dog holds still for five seconds without getting up, then increase it to 10 seconds. When your dog is holding still with very few mistakes, then take two steps away and then three.

Over several weeks of training, increase the time you ask your dog to hold the stay and the number of steps you walk away from him. When he knows the command well, you can ask him to stay when he's lying down.

TRAINING TIP

When counting seconds during training, count them as "one Mississippi, two Mississippi"—all the way up to your intended number.

Come

Coming when called is an important command for dogs to learn. A dog that runs away rather than coming when called can easily get lost or hurt.

Step 1: Put the leash on your dog. Have another person hold the end of the leash with one hand. Have a treat in your hand.

Step 2: Let your dog sniff the hand with the treat. Then take several steps away from your dog as you call him, "Buddy, come!"

Step 3: When he catches up to you, tell him, "Good boy, Buddy!" Give him the treat.

DOG DATA Always call your dog to come with a happy voice. If you sound upset or angry, your dog will not want to come because he'll think he's in trouble.

Come Across the Yard

Get another person to help you. You both need to have some treats. Have the other person hold your dog's leash. Let your dog smell the treat in your hand and then walk across the yard. Turn and call your dog, as the other person drops the leash. As soon as your dog reaches you, give him the treat and then pick up his leash. Then it's your turn to hold the leash while the other person calls him. Don't forget to drop the leash so your dog can start running.

17

Wait

When you tell your dog to stay, you go back to him to praise him. When you teach him the "wait" command, you walk away, but then call him to come to you.

Step 1: Hook the leash to your dog's collar. Ask him to sit. Hold the leash loosely so there is slack between you and your dog.

Step 2: Give him the same hand signal you did for "stay," but tell him, "Buddy, wait."

Step 3: Take a couple of steps away and then call him, "Buddy, come!" Praise him when he catches up to you.

If he gets up before you call him, tell him, "No," and have him sit again. Do steps 2 and 3 again.

When your dog understands the "wait" command and the "come" command, you can use it in other situations. At the front door inside your house, with your dog on a leash, tell him, "Buddy, sit. Wait." Then open the front door. If your dog holds still, praise him and then tell him, "OK, let's go outside," and walk outside with him. If he tries to go out before you give him permission, tell him, "No," and have him sit and wait again.

TRAINING TIP

You can use the "wait" command when someone comes to the door, so your dog doesn't dash outside.

Leave It

Many dogs get into trouble because they don't respect peoples' belongings. The "leave it" command teaches your dog not to touch something.

Step 1: Take hold of the leash close to your dog's collar. Have a treat in your pocket.

Step 2: In your other hand, have one of your dog's favorite toys.

Step 3: Drop the toy on the floor right in front of him. As you do, say, "Buddy, leave it." As soon as he looks away from the toy, give him a treat and praise him.

Step 4: If your dog tries to grab the object, stop him using the leash. At the same time, tell him, "No," and have him sit again. Then do step 3 again.

Walk

It's no fun to take your dog for a walk if he's pulling hard on the leash. Both of you will enjoy your walks more once your dog learns this command.

Step 1: Fasten the leash to your dog's collar and hold it loosely at the end. Have several treats in your pocket and one in your other hand.

Step 2: Tell your dog, "Buddy, walk."

Step 3: Hold your hand with the treat next to your dog's nose to encourage him to follow you. You want your dog to walk the same direction you're walking without pulling. If he does, tell him, "Good dog, Buddy!" Give him the treat.

Step 4: If he's pulling on the leash or trying to make you walk a different direction, hold the leash tight. Turn around and walk away from him, showing him a treat to encourage him to follow.

Step 5: If the leash tightens, don't stop. Just keep walking. When your dog realizes you're not going with him, he'll try to catch up with you. Praise him and give him a treat.

Heel

If you ever have to walk your dog on a crowded street or a narrow sidewalk, you will want him to know how to heel. When your dog heels, he walks by your side with his head next to your left leg.

Step 1: Fasten the leash to your dog's collar. Your dog should be on your left. Hold the leash in your left hand. The leash shouldn't have a lot of slack. The clip on your dog's collar should point down.

Step 2: Have some treats in your pocket and one in your right hand.

Step 3: Hold your right hand across in front of you so your dog can smell the treat. Tell your dog, "Buddy, heel," and walk.

Step 4: Use the treat to keep your dog's attention. When he's walking by your side, praise him.

Step 5: After you've walked about 10 steps, stop and ask your dog to sit. Praise him and give him the treat. Repeat steps 3 through 5 several times and then stop and play with your dog.

TRAINING TIP

If your dog still wants to pull, practice walking nicely for several days and then try heel again.

Stand

Bathing or grooming a dog that won't stay still is difficult. The "stand" command will teach your dog to stay still as you brush or dry him.

Step 1: Have some treats in your right hand.

Step 2: Have your dog on your left side. With your right hand, put the treat in front of your dog.

Step 3: Tell your dog, "Buddy, stand."

Step 4: Touch your dog under his back left leg.

Step 5: Praise him as he's standing and give him the treat.

Step 6: Tell him, "Buddy, all done!" and praise him some more. Practice this command five times in a row, then stop for a while and play with your dog.

Off

Most dogs love to lie on furniture, but no one likes to sit in dog hair. This command will teach your dog to get off the furniture.

Step 1: When your dog is on a sofa or chair, walk up to him and hook his leash to his collar. Hold the loop end. Have a treat in your other hand.

Step 2: Let him sniff the treat.

Step 3: Back away from the sofa. Tell your dog, "Buddy, off." If your dog resists, you can pull gently on his leash.

Step 4: When all four of his paws are on the floor, give him the treat and praise him.

TRAINING TIP

Only practice this command when your dog is already on the furniture. Don't make him jump up just so you can practice. That would confuse your dog.

GLOSSARY

command (kuh-MAND)—a word or phrase that tells a dog to do something

heel (HEEL)—a command telling a dog to walk by a handler's left heel

obedience (oh-BEE-dee-uhnss)—following rules and commands

praise (PRAZE)—to say words of approval

READ MORE

Gewirtz, Elaine Waldorf. *Fetch This Book: Train Your Dog to Do Almost Anything.* Our Best Friends. Pittsburgh: Eldorado Ink, 2010.

Pang, Evelyn, and Hilary Louie. *Good Dog! Kids Teach Kids about Dog Behavior and Training.* Wenatchee, Wash.: Dogwise Pub., 2008.

Rogers, Tammie. *4-H Guide to Dog Training and Dog Tricks.* Minneapolis: Voyageur Press, 2009.

INTERNET SITES

FactHound offers a safe, fun way to find Internet sites related to this book. All of the sites on FactHound have been researched by our staff.

Here's all you do:

Visit *www.facthound.com*

Type in this code: 9781429665254

Check out projects, games and lots more at
www.capstonekids.com

INDEX